# Killer Marketing Arsenal Tactics: PLR Cash

## Jinger Jarrett
http://jingerjarrett.com

# Copyright

Copyright 2013, Jinger Jarrett. All Rights reserved. You may not sell, give away or share this report. It is not free. You may print a report for your personal use.

If you need assistance, please use my convenient support desk here:

http://jingerjarrett.com/support/

Apart from any fair dealing for the purposes of research or private study, or criticism or review, as permitted under the Copyright, Designs and Patents Act 1988, this publication may only be reproduced, stored or transmitted, in any form or by any means, with the prior permission in writing of the author. Inquiries concerning reproduction outside those terms should be sent to the author.

The use of registered names, trademarks etc. in this publication does not imply, even in the absence of a specific statement, that such names are exempt from the relevant laws and regulations and therefore free for general use.

The publisher makes no representation, express or implied, with regard to the accuracy of the information contained in this book and cannot accept any legal responsibility or liability for any errors or omissions that may be made.

All resources mentioned in this ebook are listed in bold. To access the latest version of those resources, click here:

http://jingerjarrett.com/obc/myebooks/plr-cash/

# Table of Contents

**Preface** ................................................................................. **iii**
About this book ........................................................................ iii
**Introduction** ........................................................................... **1**
**Step 1 - Create A Report To Sell** ........................................... **3**
Naming Products/Buying Domains ............................................ 6
**Step 2 - Create Your Sales Site** ............................................ **13**
Create A Second Offer For Bigger Profits ................................. 18
**Step 3 - Send Traffic To Your Site And Profit** ....................... **23**
**Conclusion** ............................................................................. **27**
**Assignment** ............................................................................ **29**
**Checklist** ................................................................................ **31**
**Resources** .............................................................................. **33**

# Preface

## About this book

Private Label Rights, commonly referred to as PLR, is one of the fastest and easiest ways to get started in business online. You don't have to be a great writer to find great products to sell. All you have to do is find great PLR, update it, give it a new look, and you have a product that is uniquely your own.

The advantage is that there is an abundance of PLR material available on the internet. The disadvantage is that a lot of this PLR isn't very good. No problem. As long as you know something about your topic, you can rewrite it in your own words and end up with a great product.

That's what this ebook is about: I want to teach you how to start a business using PLR.

Don't think for one moment that a lot of marketers don't use PLR. They do. I use PLR articles for inspiration when writing my own articles. (After the first few hundred articles, you tend to get a little dry!)

Big name marketers will use PLR to create their own products if they're not using ghost writers to create products from information freely available on the internet.

The bottom line is this: if you can do a little editing, and you have a little knowledge of your topic, you can have a product in hours, not days or weeks, and begin making money this week.

Now, let's get started creating your first product.

# Introduction

Welcome to the PLR Cash Blueprint.

In this report I will outline a simple step-by-step system that you can use to create profit producing products quickly and easily.

I release new reports all the time using the exact same techniques in this report, and I'm positive you can do it too.

The best thing about this system is that you can duplicate it.

Once you have it down to where you can make money with it, you can do it over and over and over again, which will keep making you more money.

Imagine you had 20 different hot reports selling in different markets all making you money 24 hours a day. Or, if you had 20 different reports related to the same topic, and you created a membership. You gave your members a different report each month.

Not only could you make money selling the reports individually, but you could also earn a recurring income from selling them as a membership.

Work once; get paid over and over again.

It's nice to think about, but even nicer to actually accomplish.

Let's dive in!

# Step 1 - Create A Report To Sell

First, you have to find a market and create something to sell to that market.

You probably already have a market in mind that you know a product will sell in, so tons of market research generally isn't needed. (If you do need to do additional research, read the other report included in this package. I've included plenty of information on how to find a niche.)

Weight loss products sell well, as do Internet marketing products. Some markets that you may want to enter won't need extra work to see what sells. If you are unsure, I suggest going to your local grocery store and checking out the magazine rack.

If there is a market that buys products, there is a magazine for it, and going to your local grocery store's magazine rack is an incredibly easy and cheap way to do a ton of quick market research.

Nobody is going to spend the time and money to create a magazine for a market that doesn't buy anything, so the magazine publisher has already done the hard work for you.

And, there will be all kinds of ideas and web sites in those magazines that can give you ideas for your reports, and web sites to advertise on later when you have everything set up.

Plus, you can buy a few magazines and get tons of good articles/web sites/etc. for less then $20-30.

Another way to do this is to go to Amazon. Amazon offers over 80,000 magazines for sale. It's probably one of the largest collections of magazines available.

# Step 1 - Create A Report To Sell

You can search through the magazines there. Many of these magazines will also have websites, so you can visit the sites and read them instead of having to buy issues of the magazine. This will, I promise, spark plenty of ideas for you, and it won't cost you anything but some of your time.

After you have picked a topic/market for your report, you just need the content for your report.

Where do you get it? Well you have 3 options.

1. You can write it yourself. This will ensure that it is unique and is the best option.

I write all of my online business and internet marketing books posted on Amazon. Sometimes I use resale rights or PLR for digital packages I'm creating, but everything I offer has been made to be uniquely my own.

The advantage of writing your own reports is that the information is unique and exclusive. The disadvantage is that it's time consuming.

2. Or, if you swear you cannot write, then you can hire somebody else to do it. This option will cost the most but require very little time on your part.

There are plenty of ghostwriters out there who will charge a fee to write you an ebook/report/article.

Obviously it will cost more for more pages and usually the good ones will be much higher priced as well. If you skimp here and go with a cheap ghostwriter you may get a poorly written report so be careful.

Also, be very clear about what you want to avoid confusion.

## Step 1 - Create A Report To Sell

Make sure that you state how many pages you want, what the font size should be, the chapter titles, etc.

Be very specific in every aspect of the report so that whoever you hire does things your way and not theirs.

3. You can use private label content. This would be the least unique but would be cheap and would work if you are not a writer.

Here is one way you can work with private label content to make it much better. Get all kinds of private label reports, articles and ebooks on one topic, read them all, take out the best stuff from each private label item and make one "best of" report.

What this means is that you get the best information from various and different sources instead of one source where some of it is good information and some of it is bland/outdated/rehashed.

I suggest you do the same. This way, you do not have to write anything. You just copy and paste most of it into one great report.

Finding PLR products to make your "best of" report will come quite easy as they are literally everywhere. Just go to Google and type in "private label ebooks", "private label resell rights", etc. and you will see what I mean.

You are looking for private label ebooks/reports that come with sales letters. No software! Software is way too much work.

If they come with sales letters, then you do the same when writing your sales letter by making a "best of" sales letter to sell your report.

## Step 1 - Create A Report To Sell

My favorite site is, of course, **Gabor Olah's PLR Wholesaler**, and he charges a lot less for the paid option. However, you can also get a free membership valued at $197. (You'll find this on the resources site.)

You can even do this with just one PLR book. Let's say you just want to create a 20-30 page report and you got the private label rights to a 100 page ebook.

You can edit it down to a "best of" 25 page report by cutting out the 75 least helpful pages. That way your customer gets just the guts, the best parts of that 100 page book.

What do you edit?

Well since it is private label, you can charge anything you want. (It's been suggested by internet marketer Jimmy D. Brown that you charge about 75 cents to $1 per page.)

## Naming Products/Buying Domains

The first thing you change is the title. Just think up something clever, it doesn't have to be perfect.

There is a simple trick that you can use to name your products (and also use it when you buy domain names) to make it not only easy to remember, but it will also stick with people and make you somewhat unique.

It is actually a branding technique that big companies use to create a more memorable brand for their products/business.

The trick is simple, start each word with the same letter.

## Step 1 - Create A Report To Sell

For an example, how about the donut chain Krispy Kreme? While we are on donuts, how about Duncan Donuts?

(now I'm hungry)

It kind of makes it roll off the tongue better, and also of course, easier to remember.

Another trick that helps with branding is to make your product name rhyme with itself.

Use these two ideas when naming products and buying domains as much as possible.

Also, make sure to appeal to human psychology. Use words like:

- Secrets

- Breakthrough

- System

- Undercover

People love to think they are getting knowledge that nobody else has, so just naming your product something like:

Hollywood Makeup Secrets Revealed

or

# Step 1 - Create A Report To Sell

Breakthrough Bass Fishing Secrets

Just doing ideas like that can help increase sales.

Next thing you want to edit is the actual book itself. Don't worry, you don't have to write anything.

Just skim through it and delete all of the fluff and filler. The more products I sell online, the more I am realizing that people are sick of long lengthy ebooks that are filled with crap. Just cut your PLR products down to the meat - the reason why the customer paid for the book. You're won't be selling these products for a ton of money, so you don't need to have filler in it to try and increase the value.

Most PLR ebooks that you get will be in the 40-80 page range. After you get finished cutting the filler out of most books, you are left with about 20-30 pages of pure meat, which is just fine. Your customers will thank you for that.

Remember, you are looking for the best information from all of your PLR sources. It doesn't matter if you have 1 or 5 PLR ebooks/reports, get the best information from all of them and turn them into one hot report.

Also remember that you can do volumes. For instance; Let's say you found a ton of PLR stuff with lots of good information for one market.

Create a Volume 1 and sell it, then a few weeks later, release your Volume 2 to the same people who were interested in Volume 1. Depending on how much good information you have, this could go on for quite awhile making you tons of easy money!

## Step 1 - Create A Report To Sell

Another idea you may want to consider is to create product packages. If you have been online in the Internet marketing industry for any length of time, you will have seen where people take something like 10 products and bundle them into one package, and sell it cheap.

Although this is common in the Internet marketing market, it is rarely seen in other markets and works very well.

Now you don't have to bundle 10 products, just 2 or 3 would make your offer more powerful.

Whichever you decide, the point is to make it stand out from the rest a little bit.

- Change the title

- Cut the fat

- Package it with other PLR products of the same topic

- Combine

- Create new graphics

- Update the sales letter

The point is, none of this takes a lot of time. You don't have to write any new content.

Well OK, you may have to come up with new chapter names or write some "connector" paragraphs, but nothing major I assure you.

## Step 1 - Create A Report To Sell

If you were to write a 100 page ebook, it might take you days or even weeks. But to edit one will just take a few hours if you are SLOW.

You don't have to spend too much time on this. Just reading (skimming) the PLR book will tell you if it's worth selling. If it is, quickly make the changes, or cut out the best information and paste it in a new file. Then, move on to the next PLR book and do the same.

Somebody else has already spent the time editing these books once, so you just need to get in and modify the main things and be done with it.

And then, use something like **PDF995** to turn it into a PDF file and you're finished. (I use **Open Office** to edit all of my documents because my computer didn't have Microsoft Office. Open Office makes beautiful PDFs with clickable links, and you can also buy book templates for it at Lulu, as well as downloading tons of free templates at the Open Office Website itself.

Quick

Easy

Cheap

Private label is incredible for those who know how to take advantage of it, and you are now one of those people.

For those who want to write their own ebooks and books, I also highly encourage you do so. Although it does take time, it's definitely worth it because you have an exclusive product.

## Step 1 - Create A Report To Sell

Creating your own information products allows you to take all of the knowledge you have and put it into your own products, which makes it truly unique.

If you are just getting started though, PLR is a great way to do it. Once you get better at creating your products, then definitely consider writing a few on your own.

You're not limited to writing either. Audio is very popular online, as is video. You may want to consider creating these types of products as they command a higher price.

# Step 2 - Create Your Sales Site

Now that you have a new unique "best of" product, you need a site to sell it on. All you really need is a 2 page site: one sales letter and one download page. A good thing about PLR ebooks is that most come with sales letters.

Now, these aren't the best sales letters on the planet although they aren't the worst either. They are usually written by a professional copywriter, but usually a cheap copywriter. But they are certainly usable Heck, sometimes I put these sales letters up unedited and they convert at 4-5%, so you may be surprised.

All you really need to make money online is an average sales ratio, which is 1-2%. What this means is that one to two people will buy out of every 100 visitors who see the sales page.

To put it one way, marketing is a numbers game, and these numbers are the most important. You have to look at how much traffic you are getting, and how much of that traffic is buying. All of the other crap you read is just another way to make making money online more complicated than it has to be. So just focus on these two things: getting traffic, and converting it into sales.

Now, what do you do with the sales letter that came with your PLR ebook? Make it unique of course.

If you only edited one ebook into a "best of" report, then you just need to edit the one sales letter that came with it. But if you used multiple sources to come up with your report, then making a "best of" sales letter will work. Here's how to get started:

First, delete all of the graphics.

## Step 2 - Create Your Sales Site

Since you changed the name of the product already, and the graphics on the sales letter most likely have the original name of the product all over them, they have become useless. Actually, the header graphic was already useless. Header graphics decrease sales!

You don't need fancy graphics to make a sales page convert, they just look good.

The only graphic I use is an ebook cover, and since I'm branding all of my titles, the cover is similar from site to site but still different. It came from an old PLR package I purchased, and it looked so good as a cover for my books, I kept using it.

If you are like me, and you cannot create graphics, then I suggest using a software program to do them for you. There are plenty of free graphics programs on the Internet, and you can even find graphics programs specifically created to create covers for all your products.

One other thing I can suggest is that you go to **Fiverr.com**. There are some people over there who will make you an ebook cover for just $5, and you can get some pretty good stuff created there.

Next, change the headline and all sub-headlines to the color red. Red sells better than any other color.

Next you want to read it. Read the entire letter (or letters) and put yourself in the customers' shoes. Edit what you like or don't like. (Read it out loud. This will help you catch many of the grammar mistakes and make the language smoother.)

That's it really, and you're finished. I don't edit them too much because it is a waste of time. The reason is because you don't know if they are

## Step 2 - Create Your Sales Site

going to sell well the way they are. So I do the little editing that I just mentioned, then put it online and start driving traffic to it to see how well it does. You just have to try it out and see.

Sometimes it'll bring in an average sales ratio, sometimes bigger, and sometimes it'll be a flop. Those are the only things that can happen, and you shouldn't be bothered by any of them.

If it flops, its time to modify the copy somewhat, starting with the headline. Also be sure to do a search on Google to see what your competition is doing. I don't suggest taking any of their copy, but getting ideas from them isn't a bad idea.

So when you have a PLR product that flops, go around and see how other successful sales letters are written and get some ideas.

Keep a swipe file of good headlines, as well as copy that grabs you. You can refer back to this swipe file later for inspiration.

There is also pricing to consider.

As I said before, these reports will be short after you edit them, 20-30 pages or so. So your prices will be low.

Here are some good price points that work well.

- 7

- 9.97

- 14

## Step 2 - Create Your Sales Site

- 17

- 19

- 24

- 27

- 34

- 37

I usually sell these products from 7-27 dollars. That seems to be a good range for optimum amount of money per visitor.

Don't be afraid of the low price points either. $7 per sale may not seem like much but you have to remember that you will also have back end products and affiliate programs which you will sell to those customers, and those people will also be added to your customer list.

Plus, low price points will usually generate much higher sales ratios which is a good way to lead people into your sales funnel.

Okay, so far, you have not invested that much time or money. Actually, by this time, you have barely done any work at all and yet you have a product and sales letter ready to go.

Upload it to your web site and start sending traffic to it.

Do you need a domain name for it? Nope, not yet at least.

## Step 2 - Create Your Sales Site

Upload it to a domain name that you already own. For instance, if you own www.yoursite.com.

Then create:

www.yoursite.com/booktitle

If it sells without its own domain name, it will sell with one. This way, if it flops and you can't get it selling, you can just trash the idea and move on without having lost out on a domain name.

If you don't have web hosting, and you don't have any money to get started, then I would recommend these two sites, **Yola**, or **Weebly**. You can start off for free and add your domain later when you can afford it.

Both are equally good, although you can get a blog with one, so if you are interested in blogging, I would consider signing up for that one.

(I get into more detail on domains and web hosting in the list building report, so, if you need more information, read the chapter in that report.)

And believe me, don't be afraid to ditch the idea if it is becoming more work then it is worth. Sometimes these products just aren't going to sell the way you have the sales letter and product set up.

They would need a complete redo to start selling well, and with all of the different PLR products out there, it is just easier and a lot less work to ditch the loser and go find a winner.

But don't ditch the content. If it is good content and you came up with a really killer "best of" report, then you can use it for a whole host of other

## Step 2 - Create Your Sales Site

ideas, like giving it away for free to build a list or promote an affiliate program.

I have set up plenty of these PLR sites using the exact same ideas above and some just won't sell. I will modify some and if it still doesn't sell, screw it. NEXT!

It also doesn't matter if things are perfect. So many people are sitting there, working on a project for months trying to get everything perfect. Huh?? Just launch it already, nothing is perfect!

Do it fast and get it out there to sell.

## *Create A Second Offer For Bigger Profits*

Here is a good way to boost profits by 30% or more. All you do is sell another product to the person who just bought a product from you. You put this product on the thank you page.

This is a simple up sell that I'm sure you have seen a hundred times before.

So they order product A, and on the thank you page, you sell them product B.

Products A and B should be related of course.

To make it ultra powerful, call the second offer a One-Time offer and tell the customer that they will only see the sales page for product B this one time, and they will never get a chance to buy the product again.

## Step 2 - Create Your Sales Site

The scarcity and limited time factors work wonders in marketing. People equate value to things that are rare or scarce or limited. If your product is only available that one time, it will increase orders.

Again, you have probably seen this One-Time-Offer deal before if you have anything to do with the Internet marketing market. Same concept, just use it with these PLR product ideas. It works like a charm (and works better in markets outside of Internet marketing because it isn't so ridiculously common)!

This will also allow you to spend more of your profits on advertising. You can even spend all of the money you make on Product A on advertising because you will make all of your profits on product B sales. This makes getting traffic a whole lot easier.

If you don't have to make any money up front on your ads because you know you will convert 20+ percent of those customers into second offer buyers, then generating tons of traffic to your site is incredibly simple! This is what you are striving for! You can create the second report/offer the same way you created the first: with PLR!

Something else that I have used on these sales letters is video. You simply create a video of the actual product itself.

By video I mean a screen capture video using a program like Camtasia. You use it like a "Here is what you can have in minutes" idea. You call it a "tour of our product". It is very simple to do and hasn't failed yet to increase sales. It works every time.

(Since Camstasia costs about $300, that may be out of your price range. There is a free program online you can download called **Cam Studio**.

## Step 2 - Create Your Sales Site

I'll give you a quick outline of how this can be done.

1) Start up the screen cam software, and welcome the viewer to the product tour video.

2) Log in to your members area where the product will be downloaded. (If you don't have a members area and are just emailing a .PDF file to your customers to deliver your product, then just open up the file.)

3) Show the download page, discuss the bonuses, etc. Talk about everything they receive when they order and show them in the download page.

4) Show them the chapters in the book while reading some of it. This is a big part. It shows the viewer that the product is real, shows how it is presented, and they get a quick taste of exactly what is inside.

5) Thank the viewer for watching the video and remind them that they can have this within minutes from now.

Also, if you have an affiliate program, you could give them a quick glance at that and tell them they could recoup their investment by just referring two friends (or whatever, this is a simple way to make your product seem risk free!).

One last tip: it is a good idea to have some links to some unadvertised bonuses in the download area as well. Make sure to show them that and say something like "Here are some secret bonuses that I didn't mention on the product site".

Once you have the video completed and uploaded to your server, you need to link to it on the sales page.

## Step 2 - Create Your Sales Site

I have been testing this and have found that the best place is right after you list the product benefits. Before the price and guarantee.

You could also build your list with this. I haven't tried it but I'm sure that you could say:

"Subscribe today and receive a video tour of XYZ product free!" That would probably get some interest. This tactic works well, so do it every chance you get ;)

Something else you can do with this video is to submit it to the video directories like YouTube.com. (YouTube is part of Google, so you will definitely get a lot of traffic from it.)

Make sure to link back to your site in the description area to generate traffic back to your site.

This can be a quick and easy traffic generator. Search engines love video, and if you do this, you will have one to submit to the video web sites. It's quick and easy, just give it a shot!

# Step 3 - Send Traffic To Your Site And Profit

Now that you have a product to sell, and a site to sell it, you just need traffic. Although there are quite a few ways to get traffic to your website, here are some of the most effective ones you can try:

- Joint Ventures

Joint ventures are a great way to get traffic simply because you only pay for results.

And yes, you can do joint ventures with PLR content. Why would they even care? As long as it sells and it is a good quality product, then people will want to promote it.

One way to get a lot of people promoting your site is to offer huge commissions, like 70-100% and you make your money on the second offer OTO that I was talking about earlier.

You may also use Clickbank.com as your processor and use their affiliate program. You can give 75% commissions to the affiliates over there. People will promote, and take most of the first sales money, and you take all of the profits from the second sale and beyond.

Like I said earlier, if you do not have to make any money up front on the first product, then it is very simple to generate traffic.

- Pay Per Click

This is a great way to get traffic if you have the money, and you are willing to do a little testing. It's also a fast way of getting traffic, and you can have a campaign set up in as little as 15 minutes.

## Step 3 - Send Traffic To Your Site And Profit

(To help you get the most from this technique, I have included a link to a site where you can get free pay per click traffic. Hundreds of dollars' worth, so it's definitely worth looking into. Check out **Pay Per Click Search Engines** on the Resources web page.)

It is much easier and less work to just buy the traffic.

- Use PPC (and PPC doesn't just mean Adwords. There are lots of PPC advertising opportunities out there)

- Buy from web sites directly (Like the web sites who have 1st position on the PPC search engines)

- Advertise In Ezines

- Search for targeted ad networks via Google

Here is what you can do:

- Set up the web site and get it selling.

- Get some JV partners to promote it (I have yet to sell a product that other people wouldn't promote).

- Use the money made to buy ads like PPC or on web sites directly that have to do with what I am selling.

You can also use 100% limited time sales to promote these reports.

The concept of a 100% commission sale involves giving affiliates 100% of the initial sale, and making your money on the up sell and down sell.

## Step 3 - Send Traffic To Your Site And Profit

(For those who don't know what an up sell is, it's where you offer another offer on the back end, when the customer still has his/her wallet open. A down sell is a less expensive offer you make if the customer turns down the first offer.)

Here are two ways to use 100 percent commission sales:

You basically start off selling a product of some sort either using a nickel sale format where you would start the price low (like $5) and the price increases by $0.05 every 20 or 30 minutes, or you could sell the product at a fixed price of something low like $7 or $9.97.

When somebody buys, he/she is automatically enrolled in your affiliate program where he/she can promote your site and make 100% of the sale. This would be the $5 nickel sale that keeps increasing, or the $9.97 whichever you are doing. The money is instantly deposited into his/her Pay pal account. This makes it very attractive for people to promote you, so the traffic is built into the equation.

Whenever somebody buys, he/she is sent to the up sell page which sells another product that you (the owner) get all the money for. A good price point for the up sell is $27 or so, but there is no one way to do it. Make sure you test it to see what price point works best for you.

I have seen $7 up sells, and $97 up sells. It just depends on what you have to sell that is related to the first product you are selling.

The up sell page is usually portrayed as a one time offer page. The visitor only gets to see this page once and make a decision to buy or not. This creates urgency. The only way he/she can see it again is if he/she buys the first product again. If he/she does not want to buy that page, you can

## Step 3 - Send Traffic To Your Site And Profit

have a "No Thanks" link at the bottom which takes him/her to the down sell.

The down sell is another offer that is cheaper than the up sell. So, if your up sell is $27, your down sell may be $17.

Down sells are very popular in telemarketing. Telemarketers will often sell a product and then go for the up sell. If the customer says no, they try for the down sell.

You can use the $7 sales script, **$7 Secrets**, to automate all of this. It's very easy to set up, but you need your own web hosting. Since I don't own the script and ebook, I can't give it to you, but if you're interested, you can get it for about .99 over at Tradebit.

If you get some affiliates promoting your sale for 100% commissions, you can make some big money on the up sell/down sell and add hundreds/thousands of customers to your customer list.

Getting traffic isn't rocket science. Get others to promote your product for big commissions and use the money you make to buy ads on other sites and PPC.

If you are looking for the easiest way to get traffic, that would be free classifieds. I've completely covered this topic in the ebook on list building. I've also added some bonus ebooks to this package that will introduce you to some other internet marketing techniques that are highly effective but need more than just a chapter in this ebook. (You will find all these resources on the downloads page included at the end.)

# Conclusion

Now you have an outline of what to do to pump out one profit producing site after another and make some real money online.

That's it! There isn't too much to this; it is quite easy. Like I said before, stick to the simple stuff. Everybody seems to try to complicate the whole process of making money online when it is in fact quite simple.

And yes, this does require a little bit of money, and some actual work. This is a business, a real one even. It will cost something.

The good thing is, it isn't difficult, and you don't have to have any special skills. Start with the basics. I've included plenty of free resources to help you get started. Roll up your sleeves and get the work done.

It only takes a few hours to put one of these little money makers together. Just imagine if you put up one per week. At the end of one year, you'd have 52 profit centers making money for you. (You can spend the rest of the week marketing so you make even more money.) The thing I want you to remember is consistency.

Crank these PLR sites out quickly without fear of things being perfect or whatever. Some will work, some won't. Don't get discouraged by the failures, and stay positive about success! You can also increase sales with a follow up strategy or opt in email list.

There are also a few additional resources I would like to recommend that will help you make more money with this strategy.

For your payment processors, I suggest one of these: **Clickbank** or **JV Zoo**.

## Conclusion

Both allow you to offer an affiliate program. Clickbank will take care of your customer service and pay your affiliates, but they charge a one time fee of $49.95 plus a percentage of your payment.

JV Zoo allows you to list all your products for free, and then they charge 5% each time you make a sale. You can also pay a one time fee of $17. Affiliates are paid instantly.

Start an affiliate program when you are ready. I've included a copy of PayLockPro for those who want to use Pay Pal as a payment processor, and this will allow you to automate delivery of your product, as well as encrypt your payment links so no one can steal your products.

I wish you lots of success with this. If you received this product through my membership or newsletter, then please feel free to send me your feedback so I can improve this product or answer any questions you may have.

If you bought this product from my site, please post your requests on my support desk, and I'll be happy to help.

## Assignment

Build your first stream of income by creating one of these little products and building your website.

I've included a free website builder in the resources section.

Again, if you have questions, please feel free to post them on my support desk, and I'll be happy to answer your questions.

# Checklist

This checklist is provided to make sure you include everything you need to include to create each profit stream as quickly as possible.

1. Outline your title or purchase your PLR document.

2. Edit your document. Convert to PDF.

3. Edit the sales letter. Create your payment button and add this to the page.

4. Create your download page. Upload your ebook to your server and create a download link. Add this link to the download page. Test it to make sure it is working.

5. Upload all of your pages to the server.

6. If you are using PayDotCom or Clickbank, you will need to integrate your new product there so you can sell it there.

# Resources

To access the resources in this ebook, which are in bold, you will need to visit my page. This page was created so that I can offer you constantly updated resources, as well as additional bonuses. You may want to consider joining my customer list to receive notifications. Your privacy is completely protected, and I won't share your information.

http://jingerjarrett.com/obc/myebooks/plr-cash/

www.ingramcontent.com/pod-product-compliance
Lightning Source LLC
Chambersburg PA
CBHW061521180526
45171CB00001B/275